There are hundreds
and hundreds of reasons
why this book had to
be written - turn
to the back to see
just a few . . .

Vowel Consonant

Vowels:

a   e   i   o   u

Consonants:

b   c   d   f   g   h   j   k   l   m   n

p   q   r   s   t   v   w   x   y   z

Alphabetical Order

Look at the first letter of the word:

cat apple table red book

then put them in order

apple book cat red table

If the first letters are the same, look at the second letter:

help habit high huge hobby

then put them in order

habit help high hobby huge

and so on

A

Use a before a word which starts with
a consonant:

b c d f g h j k l m n p
q r s t v w x y z

a book   a pencil

or

a word which sounds as if it starts with
a consonant:

a ewe

An

Use an before a word which starts with

a vowel:

a e i o u

an apple   an umbrella

or

a word which sounds as if it starts with

a vowel:

an heir

Sounds for Spelling

a – e	cake	grapes
	flame	spade
ai	tail	brain
	against	explain
ay	hay	tray
	delay	playing
ei	eight	weight
	neighbour	sleigh

Sounds for Spelling

ee	tree	street
	sixteen	toffee

ea	meat	stream
	dream	season

ie	field	brief
	thief	chief

ey	donkey	key
	chimney	valley

y	jolly	crusty
	silky	puppy

ei	ceiling	receive
	seize	deceive

Sounds for Spelling

i – e	five	time
	slide	kite
i	mild	unkind
	blind	winding
ie	tie	magpie
	fried	satisfied
igh	flight	delight
	midnight	high
y	cry	sky
	multiply	reply

Sounds for Spelling

o – e	stone	smoke
	home	close
oa	coat	toast
	soap	groan
o	old	swollen
	roll	golden
ow	window	own
	arrow	glow

Sounds for Spelling

u – e	flute	use
	excuse	volume
ew	few	jewel
	grew	screw
ue	blue	rescue
	continue	clue

Sounds for Spelling

er	butter	term
	perhaps	clever

ir	bird	skirt
	first	confirm

ur	burn	surf
	disturb	church

Sounds for Spelling

or	for	morning
	sport	important
ar	war	wardrobe
	quarter	toward
au	fraud	haunted
	exhaust	vault
aw	straw	paw
	claw	yawn

Sounds for Spelling

ow	cow	down
	crowd	clown

ou	pound	sprout
	house	amount

Sounds for Spelling

Silent Letters:

b	comb	thumb
d	hedge	porridge
g	gnome	gnash
h	when	heir
k	knee	know
l	walk	palm
t	match	switch
w	wreck	wrist

Spelling Rules

Easy ways to remember difficult words:

b e c a u s e

big elephants can't add up sums easily

b u s i n e s s

bus in S (ess)

full at the end of a word becomes ful = helpful

till at the end of a word becomes til = until

all at the start of a word becomes al = almost

Spelling Rules

different	=	two Fs
necessary	=	one C two Ss
disappoint	=	one S two Ps
success	=	two Cs two Ss
accident	=	two Cs
succeed	=	two Cs two Es
recommend	=	two Ms
embarrass	=	two Rs two Ss
committee	=	two Ms two Ts two Es

Spelling Rules

licence (noun) A driving licence
license (verb) 007, licensed to kill!

stationary – not moving, still
stationery – paper, pens etc. (e for envelopes
            is an easy way to remember)

principal – the first or most important
principle – a basic or ethical standard

practice (noun) The doctor's practice
                opens at 8:30a.m.
practise (verb) You must practise your
                spelling!

Syllables

Syllables are the different sounds you hear in a word as you say it:

tadpole

tad   pole   =   2 syllables

caravan

car   a   van   =   3 syllables

astonishing

as   ton   ish   ing   =   4 syllables

Singular & Plural

Singular	Plural
(one)	(more than one)

+ s

sock	socks
book	books
cat	cats

words that end with a hissing sound = + es

+ es

brush	brushes
glass	glasses
fox	foxes

Singular & Plural

Singular	Plural
(one)	(more than one)

vowel + y = add s

day	days
valley	valleys
boy	boys

consonant + y = y changes to ies

berry	berries
puppy	puppies
country	countries

Singular & Plural

Singular	Plural
(one)	(more than one)

f = add s

chief	chiefs
reef	reefs
dwarf	dwarfs

f = f changes to ves

calf	calves
loaf	loaves
shelf	shelves

Singular & Plural

Singular	Plural
(one)	(more than one)

add   s   before the first hyphen

passer – by	passers – by
sister – in – law	sisters – in – law

add   s   at the end

cupful	cupfuls
spoonful	spoonfuls

Singular & Plural

Singular (one)	Plural (more than one)
	the whole word changes
mouse	mice
goose	geese
child	children
woman	women
	nothing changes
cod	cod
deer	deer
sheep	sheep
salmon	salmon

Gender

Masculine (male)	Feminine (female)
boy	girl
man	woman
uncle	aunt
king	queen
him	her
lion	lioness
bull	cow

Gender

Common (either sex)	Neuter (neither sex)
child	house
pupil	chair
visitor	river
teacher	school
friend	box
cousin	happiness
lawyer	banana

Families

Father	Mother	Baby
bull	cow	calf
dog	bitch	puppy
ram	ewe	lamb
boar	sow	piglet
billy-goat	nanny-goat	kid
cob	pen	cygnet
drake	duck	duckling
gander	goose	gosling

Rhyme

Words that rhyme end with the same sound
but not necessarily the same spelling:

cat rhymes with mat

so do:

tough   and   puff

heard   and   bird

best   and   guest

Prefix

A prefix comes before a word to change its meaning:

un   in   im   dis   ir
    il   non   mis ...

unhappy   invisible

impossible   disconnect

irregular   illegal

nonsense   misuse

Suffix

A suffix comes after a word to change its meaning:

ed   ing   ful   ment ...

play   played

dream   dreaming

hope   hopeful

astonish   astonishment

Root Words

The root is the basic word to which a prefix or a suffix can be added:

impolite (a prefix has been added)

jumped (a suffix has been added)

uncomfortable (a prefix and a suffix have been added)

Compound Words

Compound words are two separate words
which can be joined to make one word:

foot + ball = football

snow + man = snowman

moon + light = moonlight

arm + chair = armchair

Old-Fashioned Words

art	=	are
hath	=	has
hence	=	from here
hie	=	go
is't	=	is it
oft	=	often
thee	=	you
thou wilt	=	you will
'tis	=	it is
'twas	=	it was
wherefore	=	why

Diminutives

A diminutive describes something smaller:

seed	seedling
hill	hillock
leaf	leaflet
book	booklet
river	rivulet
crown	coronet

Homophones

Words which sound the same but are
different in spelling and meaning:

son   sun

knot   not

bare   bear

aloud   allowed

praise   prays   preys

Proverbs

A proverb is a wise saying usually
with a deep meaning:

Let sleeping dogs lie
(Don't stir up trouble)

Two heads are better than one
(It is often better to share your problems)

Don't count your chickens before they are hatched
(Don't be over confident about something
that hasn't yet happened)

Similes

A simile is a comparison using as or like:

as white as a sheet

as thin as a rake

as flat as a pancake

as happy as a lark

like a bolt of lightning

Metaphors

A metaphor only hints at a comparison:

You're a star.

Her face lit up.

Laura sailed into the room.

She is a mine of information.

Alliteration

Alliteration is the repetition of the beginning sound of several words in a sentence:

short sharp shock

singing softly

ruby red rose

deep dark dimples

Collective Nouns

The name for a group or collection:

a crowd of people

a herd of cows

a flock of birds

a staff of teachers

a wood or forest of trees

a posy, bunch or bouquet of flowers

Nouns

A noun is a naming word:

Proper Nouns name all the things that begin with
a capital letter:
Sunday   London   Holly

Common Nouns name all the things you can see,
hear, touch, taste or smell:
book   plum   music

Abstract Nouns name ideas and feelings:
satisfaction   happiness   intention

Collective Nouns name collections:
a crew of sailors
a swarm of bees

Pronouns

A pronoun replaces a noun:

him   we   ourselves   theirs
his   them   they ...

Henry caught the ball
He caught it

Dottie baked the cupcakes
She baked them

Charlie and Tom helped the old lady
They helped her

Adjectives

An adjective describes a noun:

a valuable antique

a deep sleep

a generous thought

a pretty , pink dress

He ate three chocolates

Comparison of Adjectives

Positive (one)	Comparative (two)	Superlative (more than two)
big	bigger	biggest
wet	wetter	wettest
good	better	best
bad	worse	worst
many	more	most
generous	more generous	most generous
beautiful	more beautiful	most beautiful

Verbs

A verb is a doing word describing action
or a state of being:

run   sleep   eat   jump
dream   stare   demolish   do

Present Tense (today)	Past Tense (yesterday)
run	ran
sing	sang
try	tried
go	went
feel	felt
buy	bought
sell	sold
say	said
find	found
swim	swam
am	was
drive	drove
speak	spoke

Adverbs

An adverb describes a verb:

He walked energetically

She slept soundly

We laughed happily

They spoke clearly

Many adverbs end in ly or ally

Some do not:

He swims well

She ran fast

They lost twice

Singular Verbs

If the subject is singular, the verb is singular:

She dances.   The dog barks.

neither of, anybody, each, nobody, every, none
are all followed by singular verbs:

Each of the children has a book.
Every one of us is invited.

If the subject is singular the verb is singular
even in a longer sentence:

Finlay, who is a good pianist, plays in a band.

Plural   Verbs

If the subject is plural, the verb is plural:

They dance.   The dogs bark.

Two singular subjects need a plural verb:

Alex and Liam are brothers.
Kit and Adam ate two huge pieces of cake.

One or more plural subjects need a plural verb:

The trees and the flowers were beautiful.

Conjunctions   Connectives

Conjunctions or connectives are words used to join two small sentences to make one longer one:

and   but   because   since   until   whenever   where   as   although   however   except   than   unless …

Louie was smiling because he had passed his exam.

Will has been at the same school since he was four years old.

I will see him before he goes to his new school.

Prepositions

A preposition shows the relationship
between one thing and another
usually indicating time or place:

Time	Place
at	above
after	against
since	through
before	beneath
during	on
until	between

Here are some more prepositions:

across along around below by for
from near of off outside over under
underneath up with without...

Preposition Correct Usage

according to

agree to (something)

agree with (somebody)

comment on

divide between (two)

divide among (many)

equal to

different from

good for

disappointed in (something)

disappointed with (somebody)

Preposition Correct Usage

off the cuff

for the most part

in the long run

at his wits' end

by all means

for better or worse

on all fours

up to the hilt

on the other hand

Capital Letters

Capital letters are used:

* for the beginning of a sentence

* for the names of people, pets, places, days, months, holidays, nationalities and languages

* for the titles of books, poems, songs, films etc

* for initials and for the word I

* for the beginning of direct speech

* for the beginning of a new line of poetry

* for words such as He, His, Him when they refer to God

Initials & Abbreviations

Use a full stop after each initial letter of:

✳   a person's name

    E . S . B . Tyrrell

✳   a company's name

✳   an organization's name

✳   an accepted abbreviation

    et cetera   =   etc.

       road   =   Rd.

Full Stops

Use a full stop at the end of a sentence.

Sentences can be statements, commands, exclamations or questions.

Statements express a fact or opinion. They need a full stop:

The dog is barking . (fact)
I think it is going to snow . (opinion)

Commands give an instruction:

Use both hands .
Do not run in the corridor .

Use a full stop unless they are.

Exclamation & Question Marks

.... commands which are short and show emotion. They need an exclamation mark:

Stop !
Don't touch it !

Exclamations show emotion. They need an exclamation mark:

What a beautiful day !
Ouch, that hurt !

Questions need an answer. They need a question mark:

Can you come to my party ?
Would you like some more hot chocolate ?

Commas

A comma marks a brief pause to help make sense of what is written:

＊ To separate words and phrases at the beginning of a sentence:

> Yes, you are in the team.
> Well, you'd better hurry.

＊ To separate a word at the end of a sentence:

> Can Mollie come over to play, please?

＊ To separate extra information in a sentence:

> Harry, who is a lawyer, lives abroad.

Commas

* Terms of address:

  Milo, come on let's go.
  We'll go to the village now, Evie.

* For direct speech:

  " I scored two goals, " shouted Henry.
  Emilia yelled, " I'll race you to the beach. "
  " I'll be back soon, "whispered Django, " just
  wait and see."

* Lists:

  We bought carrots, cauliflowers, onions,
  broccoli and potatoes.

  She was kind, warm-hearted and beautiful.

Inverted Commas

Double for speech:

" Freddie and Monty will be over soon, "
said Giselle

Single for quotations:

The poem by Robert Frost says,

'Two roads diverged in a wood, and I -
I took the one less travelled by,
And that has made all the difference.'

Inverted commas always go outside any other
punctuation:

" Shall we have scones or crumpets? "

Direct Speech   Indirect Speech

Direct Speech:

"Have you finished your homework Otto?" asked his mother.

These are the exact words spoken by Otto's mother. Direct speech always needs speech marks or inverted commas.

Indirect Speech or Reported Speech:

Otto's mother asked him if he had finished his homework.

These are not the exact words and do not need speech marks or inverted commas.

Apostrophe Possession

Singular (to show owner)

Emma's dress
The baker's shop
The dog's bowl

{ Only one Emma, baker and dog.

Plural (to show more than one owner)

The boys' cloakroom
Pets' corner
Birds' nests

{ Lots of boys, pets and birds

Irregular ones (the whole word changes)

The ladies' hairdresser
The children's playground
The policemen's radios

{ These words already show more than one owner

Contractions

The apostrophe shows where
the letters have been left out:

I am	=	I'm
you are	=	you're
he would	=	he'd
we have	=	we've
they will	=	they'll
have not	=	haven't
should have	=	should've

Two words are now one word.

Colons

A colon points ahead to something that follows. It could be a list, or to explain or summarize:

Before you go home you must: tidy your desk, collect your games kit and remember to take your homework.

Finn ran off into the bushes: he must have seen a pheasant.

It is not necessary to follow a colon with a capital letter.

Semicolons

A semicolon joins two sentences which are closely linked, perhaps where a full stop is too much and a comma is not enough:

Luca played very well yesterday; he broke his own record.

A semicolon can also be used to show a sharp contrast:

My sister hates dancing; I love it.

Don't worry. You can write very good English without ever using a semicolon!

Paragraphs

Paragraphs help the reader to understand what is written.

A paragraph is a series of sentences about the same topic.

By using paragraphs the reader will understand that they are moving from one theme to another.

Indent each new paragraph by starting to write a short distance from the margin.

Use a new line for each new paragraph.

Doubles

Use doubles to give greater emphasis:

She won fair and square.

It was left high and dry.

They raced neck and neck.

Round and round he went.

We all have our ups and downs.

Time and tide won't wait.

Only odds and ends were left.

Either   Neither

Use either and or together in a sentence:

I shall take either Serena or Zoe.

Use neither and nor together in a sentence:

Neither Alice nor John have any
more lessons today.

Your   You're

Your   =   It is your birthday party
on Saturday.

(The birthday party is yours)

You're   =   On Saturday, you're going to
a birthday party.

(On Saturday, you are going to a birthday party)

Only use you're if you mean to say you are.

It's   Its

It's   =   It is

The apostrophe shows the missing letter:

It's my turn next.
(It is my turn next)

It's time for tea.
(It is time for tea)

Its   =   possession, belonging to it.

No missing letter, so no apostrophe needed:

The dog scratched its ear.

The cat slept in its bed.

It's time the puppy had its food.
(It is time the puppy had its food)

Like   As

Use like with a pronoun:

Do you like me?

I like you.

They are like each other.

Use as with a verb:

Do as I do.

I will go for a walk as I did yesterday.

I   Me

Jane and (I , me) went for a walk.

Ignore the words: Jane and
Decide whether it is:

I went for a walk or me went for a walk

Jane and I went for a walk is correct.

The cow chased the dogs and (I , me).

Ignore the words: the dogs and
Decide whether it is:

The cow chased I or the cow chased me

The cow chased the dogs and me is correct.

Less   Fewer

Less = use before a singular word:

Less food

Less work

Fewer = use before a plural word:

Fewer lessons

Fewer people

To Two Too

To   =   I go to the shop

Two   =   2

Too   =   (as well)

          … and Max came too

      =   too hot, too sleepy

The two girls were too tired to go
any further.

There Their They're

There   =   over there

Their   =   possession

They're   =   they are

They're going there with their school bags
(They are going over there with their school
bags which belong to them)

Passed   Past

Passed   =   to pass (a verb)

He passed the ball to the goal keeper
The racing car passed all the others and
won the race

Past   =   often follows a verb

We walked past the shop
It is past nine o'clock

Golden Rules for Handwriting

* Use two hands.
  One hand holds the page, the other hand writes.

* If you are using a pencil, keep it sharp!

* Try and write neatly. There is no point in writing if it cannot be read.

Golden Rules for Story Writing

* Clear beginning, middle and end.

* Very short story line (only two or three things should happen).

* Write from your own experience.

* Don't assume the reader knows what you're writing about.

* Every now and then stop and ask yourself:

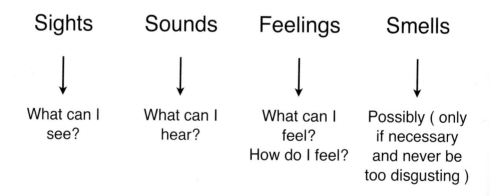

Sights	Sounds	Feelings	Smells
↓	↓	↓	↓
What can I see?	What can I hear?	What can I feel? How do I feel?	Possibly (only if necessary and never be too disgusting)

Golden Rules for Comprehension

* Read the text twice.

* Read slowly and thoroughly.

* Pick out the key word or words in the question.

* Check on the marks given for each question.

* If there is only one mark available, don't write too much.

* Make your point and give evidence from the text.

Literary Terms

Acronym	A word or letters made up from initials. (FIFA).
Antonym	Words with opposite meanings. (hot cold).
Brackets	Used to enclose an explanation or comment.
Clause	Part of a sentence with a verb.
Epigram	A witty saying. (less is more).
Eulogy	A poem praising someone.
Euphemism	A word or phrase used in place of something that might be considered too harsh or offensive.
Hyphen	Joins two words together, or one word split between two lines.
Irony	A way of being funny by saying the opposite of what you mean.

Literary Terms

Onomatopoeia	Words that sound like their meaning. (sizzle).
Oxymoron	Two opposite words that are used for special effect. (bitter sweet).
Parody	A style used for ridicule or mockery.
Pathos	Words that evoke pity, sorrow or sympathy.
Personification	To describe an inanimate object as if it were alive. (the sun smiled...)
Pun	A play on words.
Soliloquy	When a character thinks aloud.
Synonym	Words with a similar meaning. (rapid fast).
Syntax	Word order.

Here they are!

Also -

Many thanks to H and Dj for their endless
encouragement and to all those who helped
with proof reading.

If you found this book useful and would like a
few more copies for friends and relatives
e-mail:- mrsjrules@hotmail.co.uk or go to
www.mrsj.edenkent.org

5th Edition © 2008